PHOTOGRAPHY
YEARBOOK
1986

PHOTOGRAPHY
YEARBOOK
1986

Edited by Peter Wilkinson FRPS

 FOUNTAIN PRESS

Fountain Press Limited
45 The Broadway
Tolworth
Surrey KT6 7DW
England

ISBN 0 86343 077 5

Design and Layout by Grant Bradford

Typeset by Crowborough Typesetters

Printed and Bound by Graficromo S.A., Cordoba, Spain

CONTENTS

INTRODUCTION

I like to think of the PHOTOGRAPHY YEAR BOOK as being similar to a major photographic exhibition in that the pictures should be pictorially pleasing, that they should sit well together, that there should not be too much repetition of subject matter and that all accepted pictures should be of a reasonable technical quality. Obviously one would not expect all the pictures in this year's edition of the YEAR BOOK to please all the viewers, but I hope that the majority of the accepted work will be viewed with pleasure and, in many cases, admiration for the photographer and occasionally amusement.

Once again we received an excellent entry of photographs for possible inclusion, both in monochrome and in colour, from photographers, both amateur and professional, of many nationalities.

My impression, and this is borne out by the major photographic material manufacturers introducing or reintroducing a range of black and white printing papers, is that there is a very real upsurge in the interest in monochrome photography. One wonders why this should be? There is very little, if any, difference in the cost of a colour or monochrome print, and these days it is almost as easy for the darkroom enthusiast to produce prints in either medium. There are, I think, a number of reasons for this resurgence of interest. Firstly, we have become so accustomed to seeing images in colour that black and white pictures have an immediate impact; a decade or so ago this would have been the reverse and it was colour that had the impact. Secondly, by the very nature of the medium, colour photography is in the majority of cases factual or objective, any attempt to distort or control the process to any great degree for pictorial purposes immediately looks false and contrived. Many of the famous monochrome workers of the stature of the late Ansel Adams or Bill Brandt would however go to great lengths, by use of light or sometimes chemical processes in their print making to control the tonal qualities of their final prints, such control would have been impossible in colour. Thirdly, without the intrusion of the extra dimension of colour, the subject matter and the tones and the form of the picture become much more important.

With a few exceptions, most of the really outstanding photographs that I can recall from the past have been in monochrome, and there is no doubt in my mind that many of these pictures would not have been so successful had they been in colour.

When first reviewing pictures submitted by some of our more regular contributors to PHOTOGRAPHY YEAR BOOK, there are cases where their work is immediately recognisable because of either the subject matter or camera technique, or a combination of both. One's first reaction on receiving these pictures is rather like seeing an old friend in a crowd, coupled with a degree of admiration that the author of the work has developed a recognisable style, but I am beginning to question whether or not this is always necessarily good. Is it not possible that there are not examples of the photographer, having found a successful formula, being tempted to overwork that formula until their work becomes repetitive or even boring? It is not my intention to advocate that we should all suddenly change our approach to photography, but I think we should be prepared to explore the many new and exciting photographic materials, lenses and equipment readily available today, which a decade ago would have been no more than a dream. A well known and successful British professional photographer Brian Ollier, admired for his superb quality studio portraits, recently had published in the PHOTOGRAPHER some of his latest portraits where he had used 1000 A.S.A. (for the non photographic reader let me explain this is very, very fast) 35mm colour film. The inherent grain pattern of this fast material, which not even the manufacturer would recommend for studio portraiture, helped to produce pictures which were very 'different' from the usual run of studio portraiture and which had a most attractive ethereal quality.

Those of us who feel that our photography has become somewhat static should be prepared to experiment now and again and who knows what exciting pictures could result?

As photographic materials continue to improve, with the resultant high quality end product, so do the techniques used for reproducing the photographic image on the printed page, and the 1986 edition of PHOTOGRAPHY YEAR BOOK is an example of the superb quality of reproduction that is available today. It is interesting that using the latest laser scanning techniques for making the colour separations, there now seems to be little, if any, difference in the quality of reproduction from colour prints or colour transparencies.

A continuing disappointment when selecting the pictures for inclusion in the YEAR BOOK is the number of interesting pictures that have to be rejected because of poor print quality. It is impossible to make acceptable reproductions from prints which are tonally flat or over contrasty or are unsharp. Nicolas Treatt, best known for this masterful pictures of the Parisian theatre, writes in the epilogue of his book of photographs taken between 1953 and 1983 . . . "I feel it is ESSENTIAL to work as a craftsman, from the taking of the picture to the final print. The laboratory work is just as important as the act of photographing (the achievement of image quality and the print's expressive force) . . ."

Future contributors please take note!

To conclude, the publisher and I thank everyone who took the trouble to submit their pictures. Many excellent photographs could not be included purely through lack of available space. Congratulations to those whose work was accepted, and an invitation to everyone who considers that they have material which may be suitable for inclusion in the next edition to submit their pictures as soon as possible.

Peter Wilkinson, FRPS

THE PHOTOGRAPHERS

ARGENTINA

Raota Pedro Luis 134, 135

AUSTRALIA

Barnet Leslie V. 203
Pearsall Ron 24, 25, 120, 121
Tan S. 71

CANADA

Duclos Gilbert 81
Louis Pat 126
Toll Grant 222

CZECHOSLOVAKIA

Baca Vlado 158
Dostal Frantisek 84, 166
Vykulilova Alena 35, 75

DENMARK

Hyllemose Jesper 157

ECUADOR

Proano-Moreno Guillermo 139, 150

FINLAND

Niemela Erkki 222
Wallstrom Veiko 151, 202

FRANCE

Duzer Patrick 112, 130
Facchetti Paul 188
Him Christian 131, 143
Massenat P. 212
Treatt Nicolas 207

GREECE

Tsagris Athanasios 82, 195, 198

ICELAND

Thorsteinson David 50, 51

INDIA

Rajagopalan A. 215
Sodhi B.S. 64

IRAN

Shahroodi Afshin 178, 179

ITALY

Balla Giuseppe 161

MALAYSIA

Jaeook Yoo 56, 57
Lee Hin-Mun 106
Lee Soo Jong 104, 105

MALTA

Grimaud André 109

NETHERLANDS

Lybaert Daniel 29
Van den Heuvel May 78

NEW ZEALAND

London Martin 32

PAKISTAN

Ghaznavi Rooha 210, 211
Orwaisi M.R. 92, 93

POLAND

Krynicki Andrzej 36, 129

SOUTH AFRICA

Sawa Andrzej 68, 69, 170

SPAIN

Amich Albert 154
Dhers Alejandro 28
Esgueva Pablo 214
Luna Vicente J. 175

THE PHOTOGRAPHS

JAGDISH J. CHAVDA

17

PETER M. UPTON
TERRY WARR ▷

18

P. M. LOPEMAN

20

DAVID ROSS

STANLEY MATCHETT △
GEORGE AUSTEN ▷
STEPHEN CHAPMAN ▷
JOHN SMITH ▷

26

ALEJANDRO DHERS

RAINER GROSSKOPF

30

KEN DEITCHER
GUISEPPE BALLA ▷

31

WILLIAM CHEUNG

33

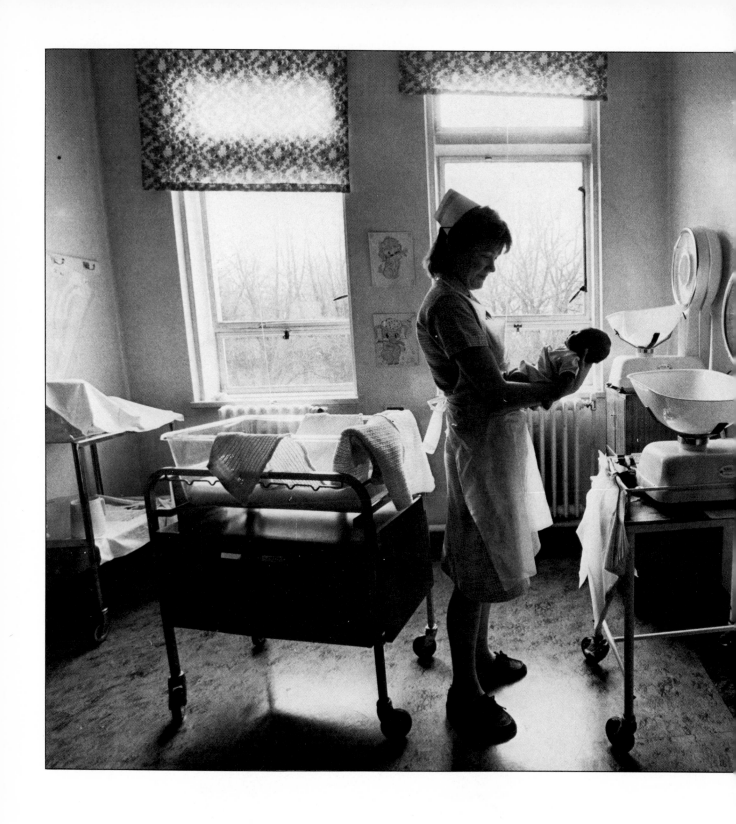

HOWARD WALKER △ ▷
ALENA VYKULILOVÁ ▷

34

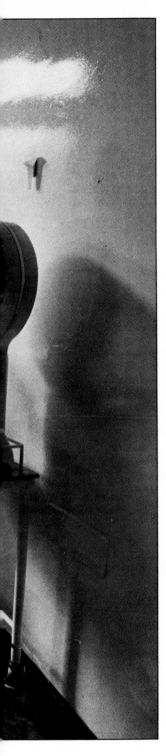

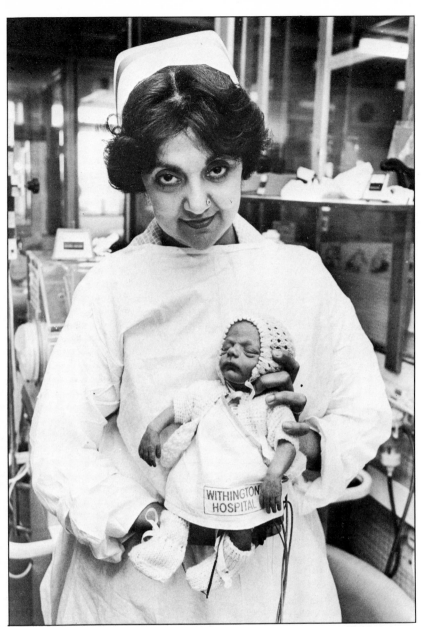

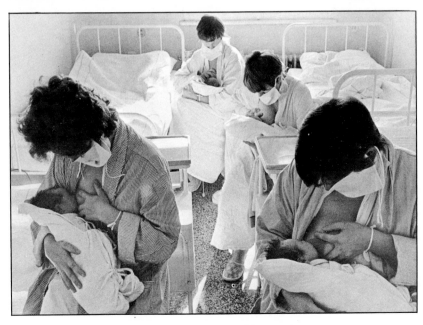

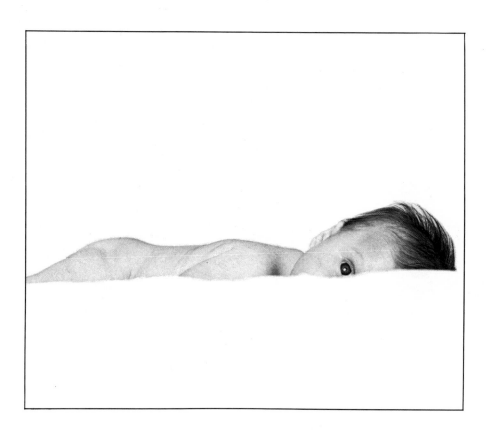

ANDRZEY KRYNICKI

T. J. RUDMAN

JANE BOWN

GERD ROMAHN

FREDERICK KENNEDY

HOWARD WALKER

ROMUALDAS RAKAUSKAS

ROMUALDAS RAKAUSKAS

45

PETER J. ELGAR

46

RAY SPENCE

47

RICHARD PEARCE

MICHAEL VARLEY

BILL WISDEN △
HOWARD WALKER ▷

52

ALAN MILLWARD

54

ANDY POLAKOWSKI

55

YOO JAEOOK

NICK JONES

58

T. J. RUDMAN

CLINE B. HARRISON

60

MICHAEL N. PARAS

61

JANE BOWN

JANE BOWN

GIUSEPPE BALLA ▷

64

ROB TALBOT △
PETER UPTON ▷

66

ANDRZEJ SAWA

69

KEITH ALLARDYCE

70

S. TAN

IAN GRIFFITHS ▷

71

G. E. BUTTON

74

ALENA VYKULILOVA

75

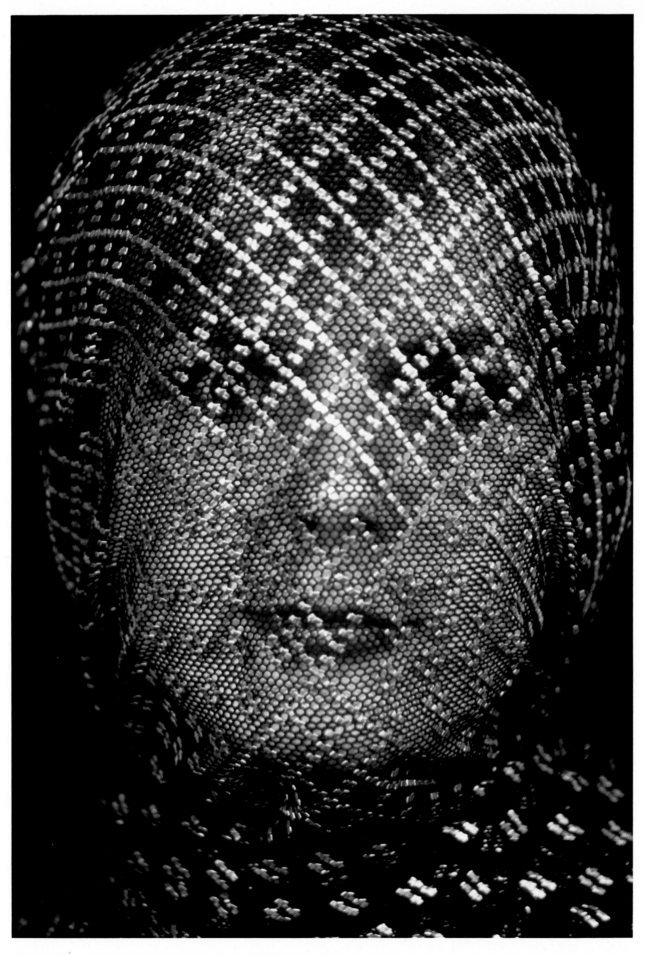

76

◁ KEITH BROWN

MIKE OKONIEWSKI
H. S. FRY

77

MAY VAN DEN HEUVEL
NEALE DAVISON

78

KEITH SAWYER

GILBERT DUCLOS

81

ATHANASIOS TSAGRIS

82

△ JOAN WAKELIN
◁ FRANTIŠEK DOSTAL

STEVE HALE

86

NEVILLE MARRINER

STEVE HALE

90

CLIVE HARRISON

91

M. R. OWAISI

92

M. R. OWAISI

HANS KÄHR △ ▷

94

HÅKAN PETTERSSON

96

MARTIN LANGER △ ▷

98

PAUL PICKARD

100

OWEN D. EVANS

MIKE TAYLOR

SOO JONG LEE

104

BILL WISDEN

106

△ ANDRÉ MICALLEF GRIMAUD
◁ NIGEL WIGGLESWORTH

109

BILL CROSS

110

STEVE HALE

111

PATRICK DUZER

STEVE HALE ▷

112

ROBIN MACWHIRTER

114

LARA ETINGOFF

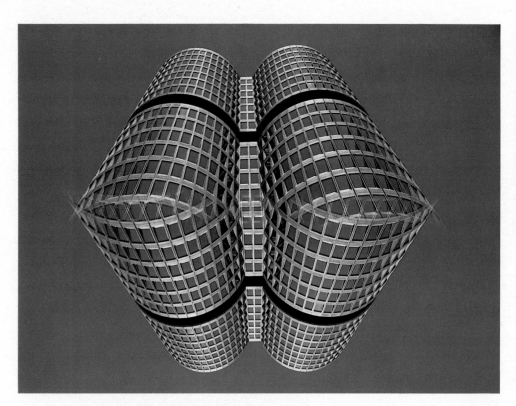

RAINER GROSSKOPF

118

DEREK REDFEARN △
RON PEARSALL ▷

119

F. P. SYMES
ARNOLD BLOOMER
◁ J. GILSENAN

123

DAVE TOASE △ ▷

STEVE HALE
◁ PAT LOUIS

127

CHRISTINE DANIEL
RONALD TYRRELL

ANDRZEJ KRYNICKI

129

PATRICK DUZER

130

CHRISTIAN HIM

DAVID HERROD

132

DAVID HERROD

133

PEDRO LUIS RAOTA

PEDRO LUIS RAOTA

135

JOHN DAVIDSON

MIKE W. BURNS

GUILLERMO PROAÑO-MORENO

139

JONAS DANIŪNAS

141

NIGEL WIGGLESWORTH
CHRISTIAN HIM ▷

142

MICHAEL VARLEY

144

W. A. J. FINN

HELENE ROGERS

146

MARGARET SALISBURY

147

NIGEL WIGGLESWORTH

148

BOB GOODE

149

GUILLERMO PROAÑO-MORENO

150

VEIKO WALLSTRÖM

151

ALBERT CLOTET I AMICH

154

CLIVE HARRISON

155

PETER DAWES

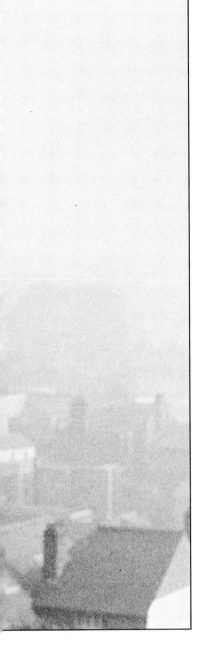

JESPER HYLLEMOSE

VLADO BACA

P. UNDERWOOD

159

JANE MILLER
ROMUALDAS POZERSKIS

160

KEITH ALLARDYCE
JOHN CHARD

161

RAINER GROSSKOPF

J. W. DETTMER ▷

162

ROB SCOTT
PIPPA KOSTERIS ▷

164

ROBERT TODD
FRANTIŠEK DOSTAL

166

F. JENDREJEWSKI
P. MASSENAT
C. F. SOUTAR ▷

167

ANDRZEJ SAWA △
ARNOLD BLOOMER ▷
PHILIP G. DYER ▷
F. P. SYMES ▷

170

BEVERLY BEAN

172

BEVERLY BEAN

173

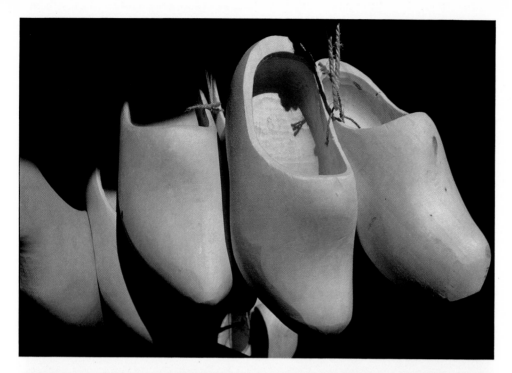

NEALE DAVISON
MIKE BIRCH

174

REINELT KLAUS △
VICENTE GENUZA △
△ THOMAS W. TAYLOR

175

MARTIN LONDON
MIKE OKONIEWSKI

176

LUCILLA PHELPS

177

AFSHIN SHAHROODI

178

AFSHIN SHAHROODI

179

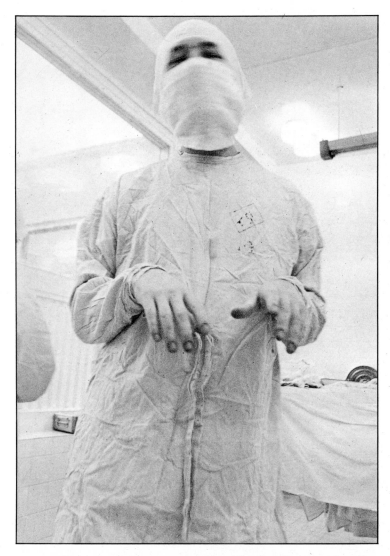

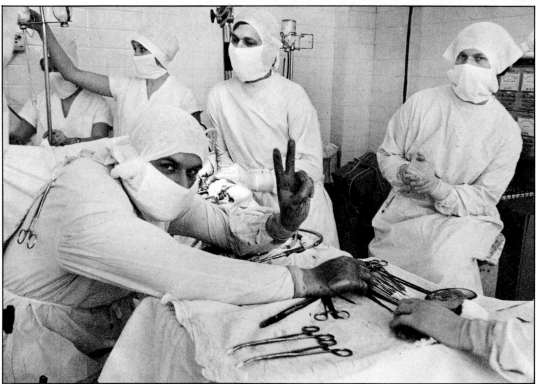

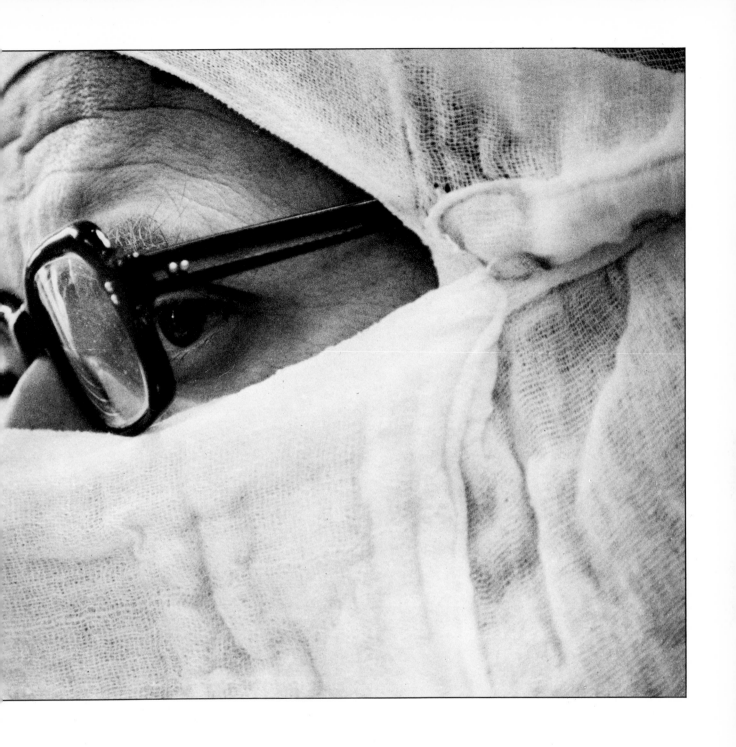

PETRAS KATAUSKAS

181

MIKE HOLLIST

184

SUE ADLER

NEVILLE MARRINER

ROMUALDAS RAKAUSKAS △ ▷

△ CHRIS TETTKE
◁ PAUL FACCHETTI

189

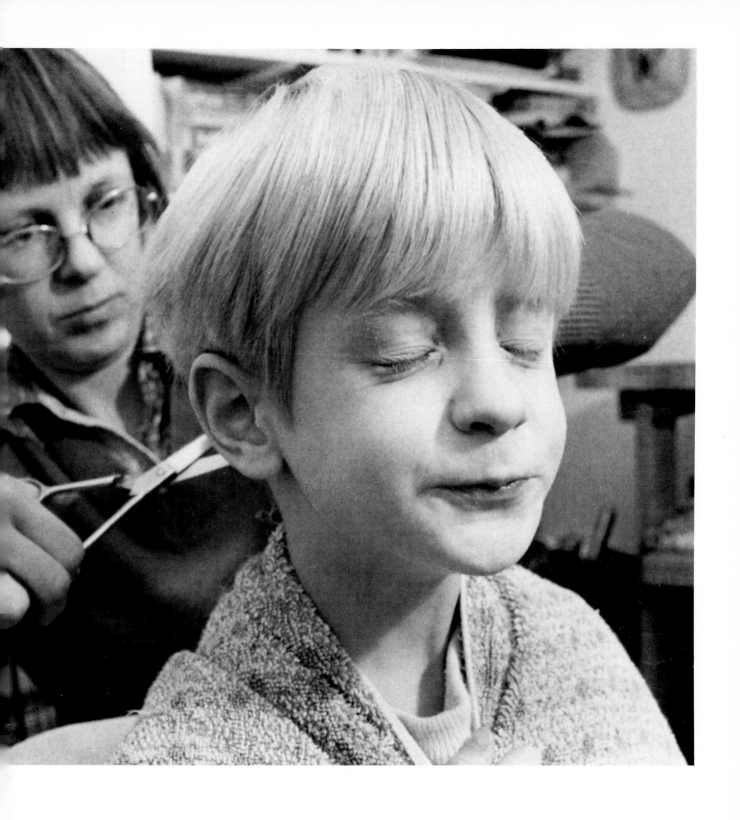

△ PETER MARSHALL
◁ L. BOND

191

△ PHILIP VALLIS
◁ NIGEL WIGGLESWORTH

193

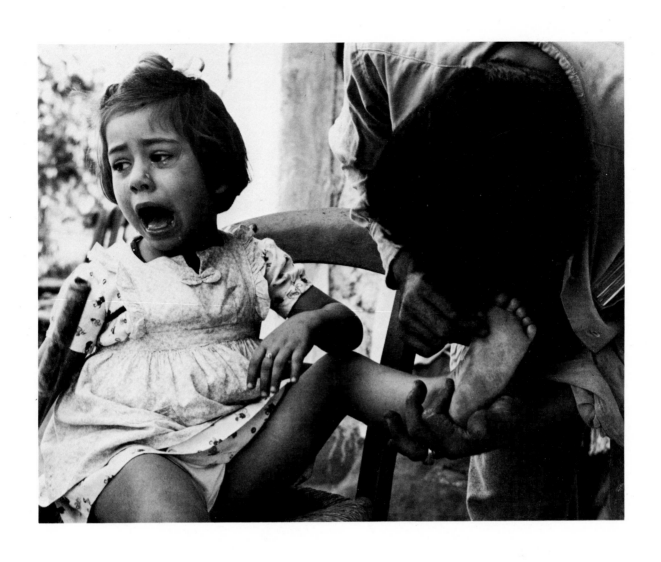

△ ATHANASIOS TSAGRIS
◁ PHILIP VALLIS

195

BOB LIGHT

196

MIKE BRETT

197

ATHANASIOS TSAGRIS

198

MARTIN LANGER △
MIKE HOLLIST ▷

VEIKO WALLSTRÖM △
LESLIE V. BARNET ▷

202

JANE BOWN

204

ALAN MILLWARD

ROMUALDAS POŽERSKIS

208

J. E. SIMPSON

ROOHA GHAZNAVI

ROOHA GHAZNAVI

211

P. MASSENAT

KEN DEITCHER
PABLO ESGUEVA

A. RAJAGOPALAN ▷

ROB TALBOT

216

B. M. WINSPEAR △
D. C. WHEELER ▷

218

D. TANN-AILWARD

▷
▽

STEPHEN M. LEE

220

ERKKI NIEMELÄ
GRANT TOLL

JOHN CHARD ▷

J. W. DETTMER

224

TECHNICAL DATA

	Front End Paper		23		30
Photographer	Owen D. Evans	Photographer	Philip G. Dyer	Photographer	Rainer Grosskopf
Camera	Pentax Spotmatic	Camera	Nikkormat	Camera	Nikon FE
Lens	85mm	Lens	200mm	Lens	25mm
Film	Ilford FB4	Film	Kodachrome 64	Film	Kodachrome 64
	17 Upper		24/25		31
Photographer	Keith Allardyce	Photographer	R. Pearsall	Photographer	Ken Deitcher
Camera	Nikkormat FT2	Camera	Nikon	Camera	Canon A1
Lens	50mm	Lens	500mm Mirror	Lens	70-210mm
Film	Kodachrome 64	Film	Fuji RD100	Film	Fujichrome 100
	17 Lower		26		32 Upper
Photographer	John Chard	Photographer	Stanley Matchett	Photographer	Martin London
Camera	Nikon FM	Camera	Nikon F2	Camera	Olympus OM1
Lens	28mm	Lens	55mm	Lens	50mm
Film	Kodachrome 64	Film	Kodachrome 64	Film	Kodachrome 25
	18		27 Upper		32 Lower
Photographer	Peter M. Upton	Photographer	George Austen	Photographer	Mike Okoniewski
Camera	Nikon F3	Camera	Pentax ME Super	Camera	Canon A1
Lens	80-200mm	Lens	80-210mm	Lens	135mm
Film	Kodachrome 64	Film	Kodachrome 64	Film	Kodachrome
	19		27 Middle		33
Photographer	Terry Warr	Photographer	Stephen Chapman	Photographer	William Cheung
Camera	Pentax ME	Camera	Olympus OM2	Camera	Mamiya RB67
Lens	135mm	Lens	80-210mm	Lens	127mm
Film	Kodak 2o0VR	Film	Kodachrome 64	Film	Kodak Tri X
	20		27 Lower		34
Photographer	P.M. Lopeman	Photographer	John Smith	Photographer	Howard Walker
Camera	Cosina CS-1	Camera	—	Camera	Leica M4
Lens	200mm	Lens	—	Lens	35mm
Film	Agfachrome 64	Film	—	Film	Ilford HP5
	21		28		35 Upper
Photographer	David Ross	Photographer	Alejandro Dhers	Photographer	Howard Walker
Camera	Olympus OM2	Camera	Nikon FM	Camera	Leica M4
Lens	50mm	Lens	24mm	Lens	35mm
Film	Kodachrome 64	Film	Kodachrome 25	Film	Ilford HP5
	22		29		35 Lower
Photographer	T. Napper	Photographer	Daniel M. Lybaert	Photographer	Alena Vykulilova
Camera	Canon AE1	Camera	Minolta XD7	Camera	Minolta SRT 303
Lens	100-300mm	Lens	28mm	Lens	—
Film	Barfen	Film	Ektachrome 200	Film	Orwo NP27

36

Photographer	Andrzej Krynicki
Camera	Pentax MX
Lens	—
Film	—

37

Photographer	T.J. Rudman
Camera	Yashica SLR
Lens	—
Film	Ilford FP5

38/39

Photographer	Jane Bown
Camera	Olympus OM1
Lens	50mm
Film	Kodak Tri X

40

Photographer	Gerd Romahn
Camera	Canon A1
Lens	28mm
Film	Agfa Pan 100

41

Photographer	Frederick Kennedy
Camera	Olympus OM1
Lens	50mm
Film	Kodak Tri X

42/43

Photographer	Howard Walker
Camera	Nikon F3
Lens	20mm
Film	Ilford HP5

44/45

Photographer	Romualdas Rakauskas
Camera	Minolta SRT
Lens	24mm
Film	NK2

46

Photographer	Peter J. Elgar
Camera	Pentax MX
Lens	120mm
Film	Ilford FP4

47

Photographer	Ray Spence
Camera	Yaschicamat 124G
Lens	75mm
Film	Ilford FP4

48

Photographer	Richard Pearce
Camera	Nikon FM
Lens	55mm
Film	Ilford XP1

49

Photographer	Michael Varley
Camera	Pentax
Lens	35mm
Film	Ilford FP4

50

Photographer	David Thorsteinson
Camera	Leica M4P
Lens	50mm
Film	Kodak Tri X

51

Photographer	David Thorsteinson
Camera	Leica M4P
Lens	35mm
Film	Kodak Tri X

52

Photographer	Bill Wisden
Camera	Canon SLR
Lens	16mm
Film	Ilford FP4

53

Photographer	Howard Walker
Camera	Leica M4
Lens	35mm
Film	Ilford HP5

54

Photographer	Alan Millward
Camera	Pentax Spotmatic
Lens	55mm
Film	Ilford FP4

55

Photographer	Andy Palakowski
Camera	Canon F1
Lens	135mm
Film	Ilford HP5

56/57

Photographer	Yoo Jaeook
Camera	Nikon F2
Lens	135mm
Film	Kodak Tri X

58

Photographer	Nick Jones
Camera	Bronica SQ-A
Lens	50mm
Film	Leica FP4

59

Photographer	T.J. Rudman
Camera	Yashica SLR
Lens	24mm
Film	Ilford FP4

60

Photographer	Clive B. Harrison
Camera	Olympus OM1
Lens	100mm
Film	Ilford XP1 400

61

Photographer	Michael N. Paras
Camera	Nikon FM
Lens	20mm
Film	Kodak Tri X

62/63

Photographer	Jane Bown
Camera	Olympus OM1
Lens	Kodak Tri X
Film	

64

Photographer	B.S. Sodhi
Camera	Pentax SPF
Lens	105mm
Film	Kodak Tri X

	65		74		80
Photographer	Jagdish Chavda	Photographer	G.E. Button	Photographer	Keith Sawyer
Camera	Nikkormat EL	Camera	Konica TC	Camera	Chinon
Lens	55mm	Lens	80-200mm	Lens	28mm
Film	Kodachrome 64	Film	Ektachrome 64	Film	Ektachrome 64

	66		75		81
Photographer	Rob Talbot	Photographer	Alena Vykulilova	Photographer	Gilbert Duclos
Camera	Nikon F3	Camera	Minolta SRT 303	Camera	Rollei 35S
Lens	180mm	Lens	50mm	Lens	—
Film	Ektachrome	Film	Kodachrome 64	Film	Ilford FP4

	67		76		82
Photographer	Steve Hale	Photographer	Keith Brown	Photographer	Athanasios Tsagris
Camera	Nikon	Camera	Minolta XGM	Camera	Hasselblad
Lens	400mm	Lens	70-210mm	Lens	500mm
Film	Kodachrome 64	Film	Ektachrome 100	Film	Ilford HP5

	68		77 Upper		83
Photographer	Andrzej Sawa	Photographer	Mike Okoniewski	Photographer	David Bartram
Camera	Nikon FE	Camera	Canon A1	Camera	Rolleiflex
Lens	400mm	Lens	400mm	Lens	80mm
Film	—	Film	Kodachrome 64	Film	Ilford FP4

	69		77 Lower		84
Photographer	Andrzej Sawa	Photographer	H.S. Fry	Photographer	Frantisek Dostal
Camera	Nikon FA	Camera	Nikon F3	Camera	Minolta SRT 303
Lens	80-200mm	Lens	80-200mm	Lens	35mm
Film	—	Film	Kodachrome 64	Film	Orwo NP22

	70		78 Upper		85
Photographer	Keith Allardyce	Photographer	May Van den Heuvel	Photographer	Joan Wakelin
Camera	Nikkormat FT2	Camera	Nikon F3	Camera	Canon AE1
Lens	50mm	Lens	135mm	Lens	35-70mm
Film	Kodachrome 64	Film	Agfa 50S	Film	Ilford FP4

	71		78 Lower		86
Photographer	S. Tan	Photographer	Neale Davison	Photographer	Steve Hall
Camera	Nikon FM	Camera	Pentax SP	Camera	Nikon
Lens	24mm	Lens	55mm	Lens	50mm
Film	Kodachrome 25	Film	Ektachrome	Film	Kodak Tri X

	72/73		79		87
Photographer	Ian Griffiths	Photographer	Beverly Bean	Photographer	Mike Brett
Camera	Nikon FE	Camera	Mamiya	Camera	Nikon FM2
Lens	24mm	Lens	210mm	Lens	300mm
Film	Ektachrome 200	Film	Kodacolor 2	Film	Ilford XP1

	88/89		98 Upper		106
Photographer	Neville Marriner	Photographer	Martin Langer	Photographer	Bill Wisden
Camera	Nikon F3	Camera	Nikon F2	Camera	Canon SLR
Lens	300mm	Lens	35mm	Lens	70-150mm
Film	Kodak Tri X	Film	Kodak Tri X	Film	Ilford FP4

	90		98 Lower		107
Photographer	Steve Hale	Photographer	Martin Langer	Photographer	Hin-Mun Lee
Camera	Nikon	Camera	Nikon F2	Camera	Pentax Spotmatic
Lens	35mm	Lens	24mm	Lens	135mm
Film	Kodak Tri X	Film	Kodak Tri X	Film	Kodax Plus X

	91		99		108
Photographer	Clive B. Harrison	Photographer	Martin Langer	Photographer	Nigel Wigglesworth
Camera	Olympus OM1	Camera	Nikon F2	Camera	Nikkormat
Lens	50mm	Lens	24mm	Lens	24mm
Film	Ilford XP1 400	Film	Kodak Tri X	Film	—

	92/93		100		109
Photographer	M.R. Orwaisi	Photographer	Paul Pickard	Photographer	Andrré Grimaud
Camera	Nikon FM2	Camera	Nikon FM	Camera	Ricoh KR-10
Lens	80-210mm	Lens	135mm	Lens	135mm
Film	Ilford HP5	Film	Kodak Tri X	Film	Agfa Pan 100

	94		101		110
Photographer	Hans Kähr	Photographer	Neville Marriner	Photographer	Bill Cross
Camera	Nikon F2	Camera	Nikon F3	Camera	Nikon
Lens	55mm	Lens	24mm	Lens	135mm
Film	Kodak Tri X	Film	Kodak Tri X	Film	Kodak Tri X

	95		102		111
Photographer	Hans Kähr	Photographer	Owen D. Evans	Photographer	Steve Hale
Camera	Nikon F2	Camera	Pentax Spotmatic	Camera	Nikon
Lens	50-250mm	Lens	24mm	Lens	50mm
Film	Kodak Tri X	Film	Ilford FP4	Film	Kodak Tri X

	96		103		112
Photographer	Hakan Pettersson	Photographer	Mike Taylor	Photographer	Patrick Duzer
Camera	Leicaflex SL	Camera	Canon A1	Camera	Nikon F
Lens	50mm Summicron	Lens	70-210mm	Lens	105mm
Film	Ilford Pan F	Film	Kodachrome HP5	Film	Kodak Tri X

	97		104/105		113
Photographer	Hakan Pettersson	Photographer	Soo Jong Lee	Photographer	Steve Hale
Camera	Leicaflex SL	Camera	Nikon F	Camera	Nikon
Lens	35mm Summicron	Lens	105mm	Lens	400mm
Film	Kodak Plus X	Film	Kodak Tri X	Film	Kodachrome 64

	114 Upper		122		129 Upper
Photographer	Robin Macwhirter	Photographer	J. Gilsenan	Photographer	Andrzej Krynicki
Camera	Pentax K1000	Camera	Zenith	Camera	Pentax 6x6
Lens	50mm	Lens	135mm	Lens	35mm
Film	Kodachrome 64	Film	Kodachrome 64	Film	Kodak Tri X

	114 Lower		123 Upper		129 Lower
Photographer	Robin Macwhirter	Photographer	F.P. Symes	Photographer	Andrzej Krynicki
Camera	Pentax K1000	Camera	Nikon F3	Camera	Pentax MX
Lens	70-150mm	Lens	80-200mm	Lens	15mm
Film	Kodachrome 64	Film	Ektachrome 64	Film	Kodak Tri X

	115		123 Lower		130
Photographer	Robin Macwhirter	Photographer	Arnold Bloomer	Photographer	Patrick Duzer
Camera	Pentax K1000	Camera	Nikkormat FT3	Camera	Nikon F
Lens	70-150mm	Lens	135mm	Lens	180mm
Film	Kodachrome 64	Film	Barfen	Film	Kodak Tri X

	116		124/125		131
Photographer	Lara Etingoff	Photographer	David Toase	Photographer	Christian Him
Camera	Canon A1	Camera	Minolta XD7	Camera	Olympus OM2
Lens	55mm	Lens	100mm	Lens	24mm
Film	Ektachrome	Film	Kodachrome 25	Film	Kodak Tri X

	117		126		132
Photographer	Kip Rano	Photographer	Pat Louis	Photographer	David Herrod
Camera	—	Camera	Nikon F3	Camera	Mamiya 645
Lens	—	Lens	180mm	Lens	110mm
Film	Kodachrome	Film	Kodachrome 25	Film	Ilford FP4

	118		127		133
Photographer	Rainer Grosskopf	Photographer	Steve Hale	Photographer	David Herrod
Camera	NikonFE	Camera	Nikon	Camera	Nikon FE2
Lens	24mm	Lens	300mm	Lens	135mm
Film	Ektachrome 100	Film	Kodachrome 64	Film	Ilford FP4

	119		128		134/135
Photographer	Derek Redfearn	Photographer	Christine Daniel	Photographer	Pedro Luis Raota
Camera	Canon A1	Camera	Olympus OM10	Camera	Hasselblad
Lens	100mm	Lens	50mm	Lens	4/150mm Connar
Film	Kodachrome 64	Film	Kodachrome	Film	Kodak Tri X

	120/121		128 Lower		136/137
Photographer	Ron Pearsall	Photographer	Ronald Tyrrell	Photographer	John Davidson
Camera	Nikon	Camera	Contax	Camera	Nikon F2
Lens	500mm mirror	Lens	50mm	Lens	600mm
Film	Fuji RD100	Film	Kodachrome 25	Film	Kodak Tri X

	138		145		153
Photographer	Mike W. Burns	Photographer	W.A.J. Finn	Photographer	Werner Kohn
Camera	Pentax MX	Camera	Olympus OM2	Camera	Nikon FE
Lens	100mm	Lens	200mm	Lens	180mm
Film	Ilford FP4	Film	Kodak Plus X	Film	Ilford FP4

	139		146		154
Photographer	G. Proano-Moreno	Photographer	Helen Rogers	Photographer	Albert C. Amich
Camera	Rolleicord	Camera	Canon F1	Camera	Nikon F
Lens	75mm	Lens	135mm	Lens	50mm
Film	Kodak Verichrome Pan	Film	Ilford XP1 800	Film	Kodak Plus X

	140 Upper		147		155
Photographer	Jonas Daniunas	Photographer	Margaret Salisbury	Photographer	Clive B. Harrison
Camera	Minolta X700	Camera	Pentax SP500	Camera	Olympus OM1
Lens	28-85mm	Lens	28mm	Lens	28mm
Film	A-Z w	Film	Ilford FP4	Film	Ilford XP1 400

	140 Lower		148		156
Photographer	Jonas Daniunas	Photographer	Nigel Wigglesworth	Photographer	Peter Dawes
Camera	Minolta X700	Camera	Nikon F2	Camera	NikonF2A
Lens	2.-35mm	Lens	70-120mm	Lens	50mm
Film	A-Z w	Film	—	Film	Kodak Tri X

	141		149		157
Photographer	Jonas Daniunas	Photographer	Bob Goode	Photographer	Jesper Hyllemose
Camera	Fed 4	Camera	Nikon FM	Camera	Pentax K2
Lens	28mm	Lens	90mm	Lens	28mm
Film	KN-3	Film	Ilford FP4	Film	Ilford HP5

	142		150		158
Photographer	Nigel Wigglesworth	Photographer	G. Froano-Moreno	Photographer	Vlado Baca
Camera	Nikon F2	Camera	Rolleicord	Camera	Canon F1
Lens	50mm	Lens	75mm	Lens	80-200mm
Film	—	Film	Kodak Verichrome Pan	Film	Ilford HP5

	143		151		159
Photographer	Christian Him	Photographer	Veiko Wallström	Photographer	P. Underwood
Camera	Olympus OM2	Camera	Nikon	Camera	Minolta XD7
Lens	24mm	Lens	20mm	Lens	80-210mm
Film	Kodak Tri X	Film	Kodak Tri X	Film	Ilford FP4

	144		152		160 Upper
Photographer	Michael Varley	Photographer	Werner Kohn	Photographer	Jane Miller
Camera	Chinon CE4	Camera	Nikon FE	Camera	Mamiya C330
Lens	135mm	Lens	28mm	Lens	80mm
Film	Ilford FP4	Film	Ilford FP4	Film	Kodak Tri X

	160 Lower		167		174 Lower
Photographer	Romualdas Pozerskis	Photographer	F. Jendrejenski	Photographer	Mike Birch
Camera	Minolta SET-102	Camera	Minolta XD7	Camera	Nikon F2
Lens	24mm	Lens	35mm	Lens	28-45mm
Film	KN3	Film	Kodachrome 64	Film	Fujichrome 100

	161		168/169		175 Upper
Photographer	Giuseppe Balla	Photographer	C.F. Soutar	Photographer	Klaus Reinelt
Camera	—	Camera	—	Camera	Nikon FE
Lens	—	Lens	—	Lens	28mm
Film	—	Film	—	Film	Kodachrome 64

	162		170		175 Lower left
Photographer	Rainer Grosskopf	Photographer	Andrzej Sawa	Photographer	Thomas W. Taylor
Camera	Nikon FE	Camera	Nikon FA	Camera	Canon EF
Lens	80-200mm	Lens	300mm	Lens	24mm
Film	Ektachrome 100	Film	Kodachrome 64	Film	Ektachrome 200

	163		171 Upper		175 Lower right
Photographer	J.W. Dettmer	Photographer	Arnold Bloomer	Photographer	Vincente J. Luna
Camera	Nikon F3	Camera	Nikkormat FT3	Camera	Yaschica FX-3
Lens	55mm	Lens	135mm	Lens	28mm
Film	Ektachrome 64	Film	Barfen CR100	Film	Peruchrome C19

	164		171 Middle		176
Photographer	Rob Scott	Photographer	Philip G. Dyer	Photographer	Giuseppe Balla
Camera	Nikon FE	Camera	Nikkormat	Camera	—
Lens	80-210mm	Lens	200mm	Lens	—
Film	Kodachrome 64	Film	Kodachrome 64	Film	—

	165		171 Lower		177
Photographer	Pippa Kostoris	Photographer	F.P. Symes	Photographer	Lucilla Phelps
Camera	Olympus XA2	Camera	Nikon FE	Camera	Hasselblad
Lens	35mm	Lens	80-200	Lens	50mm
Film	Kodachrome 64	Film	Ektachrome 64	Film	Kodak Plus X

	166 Upper		172/173		178
Photographer	Robert Todd	Photographer	Beverly Bean	Photographer	Afshin Shahroodi
Camera	Canon A1	Camera	Mamiya 645	Camera	Olympus OM2
Lens	100mm	Lens	80mm	Lens	24mm
Film	Ektachrome 64	Film	Kodak VR3	Film	Orwer 125

	166 Lower		174 Upper		179
Photographer	Frantisek Dostal	Photographer	Neale Davison	Photographer	Afshin Shahroodi
Camera	Minolta SRT	Camera	Pentax SP111	Camera	Olympus OM2
Lens	24mm	Lens	55mm	Lens	50mm
Film	Ektachrome 200	Film	Kodachrome 64	Film	Agfa Isopan 125

180 Upper
Photographer: Petras Katauskas
Camera: Canon AE1
Lens: 35-70mm
Film: Foto 250

180 Lower
Photographer: Petras Katauskas
Camera: Canon AE1
Lens: 28mm
Film: Foto 250

181
Photographer: Petras Katauskas
Camera: Canon A1
Lens: 70-210mm
Film: Foto 250

182/183
Photographer: Mike Hollist
Camera: Nikon F2
Lens: 85mm
Film: —

184
Photographer: Sue Adler
Camera: Canon F
Lens: —
Film: Kodak Tri X

185
Photographer: Neville Marriner
Camera: Nikon F3
Lens: 50mm
Film: Kodak Tri X

186/187
Photographer: R. Rakauskas
Camera: Minolta SET
Lens: 24mm
Film: NK2

188
Photographer: Paul Facchetti
Camera: Hasselblad
Lens: —
Film: Ilford HP5

189
Photographer: Chris Tettke
Camera: Konica FS1
Lens: 50mm
Film: Agfa Pan 100

190
Photographer: L. Bond
Camera: Canon AE1
Lens: 135mm
Film: Ilford FP4

191
Photographer: Peter Marshall
Camera: Olympus OM1
Lens: 35mm
Film: Kodak Tri X

192
Photographer: N. Wigglesorth
Camera: Nikon F2
Lens: 24mm
Film: —

193
Photographer: Philip Vallis
Camera: Rolleiflex
Lens: 80mm
Film: Ilford HP5

194
Photographer: Philip Vallis
Camera: Mamiya 645
Lens: 150mm
Film: Ilford HP5

195
Photographer: Athanasios Tsagris
Camera: Hasselblad
Lens: 50mm
Film: Ilford HP5

196
Photographer: Bob Light
Camera: Canon AL1
Lens: 200mm
Film: Kodak Tri X

197
Photographer: Mike Brett
Camera: Nikon F2
Lens: 300mm
Film: Ilford XP1

198
Photographer: Athanasios Tsagris
Camera: Hasselblad
Lens: 500mm
Film: Ilford HP5

199
Photographer: Martin Langer
Camera: —
Lens: —
Film: —

200/201
Photographer: Mike Hollist
Camera: Nikon F2
Lens: 180mm
Film: —

202
Photographer: Veiko Wallström
Camera: Nikon FE
Lens: 80mm
Film: Kodak Tri X

203
Photographer: Leslie V. Barnet
Camera: Hasselblad C500
Lens: 150mm
Film: Ilford FP4

204
Photographer: Jane Bown
Camera: Olympus OM1
Lens: 28mm
Film: Kodak Tri X

205
Photographer: Eddie Brown
Camera: Nikon F2
Lens: 200mm
Film: Kodak Tri X

206

Photographer	Alan Millward
Camera	Pentax Spotmatic
Lens	55mm
Film	Kodak Tri X

207

Photographer	Nicolas Treatt
Camera	—
Lens	—
Film	—

208

Photographer	R. Pozerskis
Camera	Minolta XD 11
Lens	35mm
Film	160 ASA

209

Photographer	J.E. Simpson
Camera	Nikon FM
Lens	135mm
Film	Kodachrome 25

210/211

Photographer	Rooha Ghaznavi
Camera	Nikon F3
Lens	105mm
Film	Fujichrome 100

212

Photographer	P. Massenat
Camera	—
Lens	—
Film	—

213

Photographer	Ron Davies
Camera	Olympus OM2
Lens	85mm
Film	3M 1000

214 Upper

Photographer	Ken Deitcher
Camera	Canon A1
Lens	70-210mm
Film	Fujichrome 100

214 Lower

Photographer	Pablo Esgueva
Camera	Olympus OM2
Lens	80mm
Film	Ektachrome 64

215

Photographer	A. Rajagopalan
Camera	Nikon FE
Lens	80-210
Film	Kodachrome 64

216

Photographer	Rob Talbot
Camera	Nikon F3
Lens	16mm
Film	Kodachrome 64

217

Photographer	Rob Talbot
Camera	Nikon F3
Lens	300mm
Film	Kodachrome 64

218 Upper

Photographer	B.M. Winspear
Camera	35mm
Lens	—
Film	Kodachrome

218 Lower

Photographer	D.C. Wheeler
Camera	Pentax LX
Lens	24-35mm
Film	Kodachrome

219 Upper

Photographer	D. Tann-Ailward
Camera	Canon
Lens	35-105mm
Film	Kodachrome 64

219 Lower

Photographer	D. Tann-Ailward
Camera	Canon
Lens	100-300mm
Film	Kodachrome 64

220

Photographer	Stephen Lee
Camera	Pentax
Lens	40mm
Film	Agfachrome 64

221

Photographer	Peter Wilkinson
Camera	Pentacon Six
Lens	50mm
Film	Agfacolor 100

222 Upper

Photographer	Erkki Niemela
Camera	Leicaflex SL2
Lens	Kodachrome 25
Film	

222 Lower

Photographer	Grant Toll
Camera	Nikon
Lens	50mm
Film	Kodachrome 25

223

Photographer	John Chard
Camera	Nikon FM
Lens	28mm
Film	Kodachrome 64

224

Photographer	J.W. Dettmer
Camera	Nikon F3
Lens	55mm
Film	Ektachrome 64

Rear End Paper

Photographer	Peter M. Rees
Camera	Olympus OM1
Lens	28mm
Film	Kodak 1R